PERFECT BOWLAND

Perfect
BOWLAND

ANDY STANSFIELD

HALSGROVE

First published in Great Britain in 2008

British Library Cataloguing-in-Publication Data
A CIP record for this title is available from the British Library

ISBN 978 1 84114 738 3

HALSGROVE
Halsgrove House
Ryelands Industrial Estate
Bagley Road, Wellington, Somerset TA21 9PZ
Tel: 01823 653777   Fax: 01823 216796
email: sales@halsgrove.com
website: www.halsgrove.com

Printed and bound by
Grafiche Flaminia, Italy

INTRODUCTION

For the uninitiated, the Forest of Bowland is located to the east of Lancaster and immediately to the south of the Yorkshire Dales National Park. Despite its proximity to the Dales, it has a different geological history and consequently provides a very different visual experience. The area is accessed readily from the M6 to the west and from the A59 or M65 to the south. The Forest of Bowland lies predominantly or entirely in Lancashire, depending on how you define its area.

There are three different areas which can be called the Forest of Bowland. The first, smallest and oldest is the medieval royal hunting reserve which was relatively tiny in area and which is obviously no longer applicable. The largest is the Forest of Bowland Area of Outstanding Natural Beauty (AONB) which was designated in 1964, has a clearly defined boundary, and covers over 300 square miles. As well as including Pendle Hill as an outlier to the south-east, it extends

a long way northwards to the River Lune and includes the northern valleys of the Roeburn and Hindburn, stretching almost to Settle. It is this larger area which defined the content of my first book *The Forest of Bowland & Pendle Hill: An Area of Outstanding Natural Beauty*, also published by Halsgrove.

The third definition of the area is the colloquial one, which falls between the previous two in size, and has no clear boundary. If anything, it is defined by people's intent when they say that they are going to visit the Forest of Bowland and consists of the area shown on the map at the front of this book. It is this area which is covered by the photographs which follow.

One of the greatest pleasures in my life is visiting somewhere new and the photographic opportunities and challenges which that brings. So, in some ways, I find it odd that the Forest of Bowland should invoke those same feelings each time I visit it, having done so countless times in the past and especially during the last three years. Yet it continues to excite me and each visit gives rise to completely new subject matter as well as different treatments of subjects I have photographed before.

I have my favourite places, of course, and refer to some of them in the captions which follow. Then there are those special locations, treasured memories that are deeply personal, which I don't write about. All travel writers have such places, ones that they refuse to share with their readers for fear that too many new visitors will break the spell and somehow ruin the memories they hold.

When I completed what seemed a mammoth task in writing my first book on the area, I felt that there was so much more waiting to be revealed, hence this second book. I still feel that way and hope that more books may follow. One day, perhaps, I will feel that I have communicated all the depth of character, the history, the beauty and the harshness, the folklore and the mysteries of the Forest of Bowland — but somehow I very much doubt it. For one thing, it is essentially a vast organism that evolves every day and so never reaches completion.

Of the hundreds of photographs I have taken around Bowland, the selection used for this book is a deeply personal one and reflects my current interests. In particular, I was conscious that everyone describes the Forest of Bowland as not being a forest in the woodland sense but a former royal hunting reserve, with the term 'forest' retaining its medieval meaning. As a result, the trees and ancient woodlands of the area tend to be down-played and I was determined to remedy this. Consequently, you will find a strong woodland theme running through the subject matter.

The success of this book will be determined not by its sales but by its impact on you, the reader. If it prompts you to visit Bowland for the first time, it will have been an outstanding success because I know that you will visit again and again. If you are already broadly familiar with the area but use this book as a prompt to discover new places and new experiences, it will have been equally successful, though in a different way. And if you simply use it to invoke memories of past visits because you now live far away, then I hope it serves you well and that, one day, you will return.

Andy Stansfield

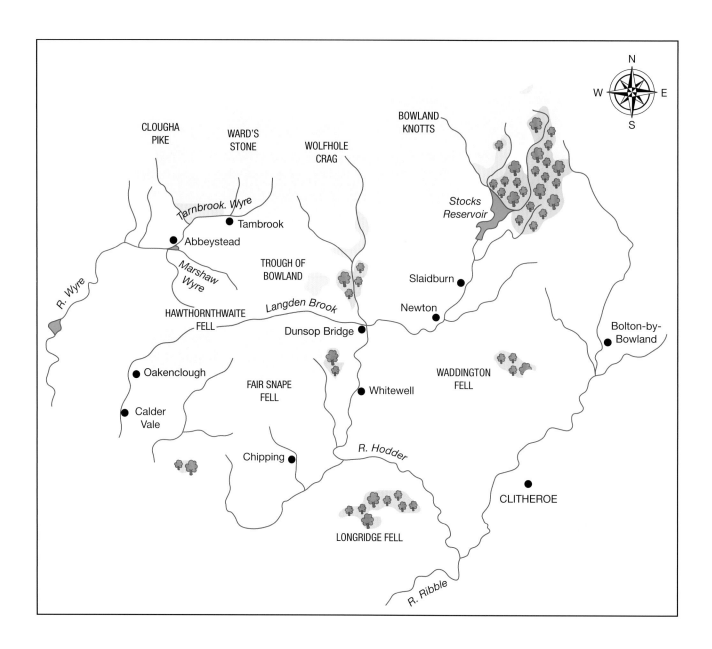

The secret garden
Most first-time visitors to the Forest of Bowland find that it comes as a complete surprise, like discovering a gate into a secret garden. Not sure what to expect, they tentatively creak open the gate and start to discover layer after layer of scenic variety. Turning the pages of this book, I hope, will be much the same process.

Trough of Bowland

The Trough itself is a small nick in the hills through which an ancient road winds its way over the pass from Dunsop Bridge to Lancaster. This is a late afternoon view from just below the pass looking back towards Dunsop Bridge and Totridge.

Spring lambs
Despite the ravages of Foot and Mouth Disease earlier this decade, sheep are still the mainstay for the area's farmers.
These spring lambs are grazing in the Hodder valley with Birkett Fell in the background.

Bolton Peel
This magnificent farm, with its cross and the remains of a moat, lies just outside the ancient village of Bolton-by-Bowland in the south-east corner of the Area of Outstanding Natural Beauty.

Langden Castle

Halfway between Dunsop Bridge and the Trough, a United Utilities access road follows Langden Brook westwards from the road, giving way to a track which leads into one of the bleakest parts of Bowland. Guided walks run by the RSPB use this route for their birds of prey identification walk as you can hope to see buzzards, merlins and hen harriers on a good day.

Marshaw Wyre

One of the two tributaries feeding the River Wyre, the other being Tarnbrook Wyre; here it is a gentle stream adjacent to the road on the west side of the Trough. Its banks provide a popular picnic venue, especially in summer.

Tree bole
The remarkable split in the bole of this tree has led to long discussions at home about what might have caused it, without reaching any firm conclusions. What I can say is that it made an interesting subject to photograph!

Tree bark
The mixture of moss, lichen and flaking bark with soft shadows from the diffuse sunlight caught my eye for this close-up.

Cobbled path, Newton in Bowland
The village streets have long since been resurfaced but, here and there, you'll still find stretches of cobbled footpath dating back hundreds of years. Little used, this one has delicate flowers and weeds which have managed to take root and which complement the relatively tiny cobbles.

Opposite: **The boar's head**
You might expect to find this dramatic wall decoration outside an aptly named pub, but it is actually to be found at Bowland Wild Boar Park near the village of Chipping. This is a popular visitor attraction, especially with children, where they can also feed the deer.

Dunsop Bridge

This tiny village lies not just at the heart of Bowland but virtually at the centre of the UK, the precise spot being fractionally north west of Whitendale Hanging Stones, a remote moorland location just over four miles north of the village. In 1992 BT located its 100,000th phone box in the village, just beyond the parked car in the distance. Puddleducks (left) is the affectionate name for the village Post Office and tea rooms.

20

Happy Birthday Ma'am
Her Majesty the Queen visiting Dunsop Bridge and her Duchy of Lancaster estate during
her 80th birthday celebrations. She later had lunch at The Inn at Whitewell.

Ivy-leaved toadflax
This delicately-flowered plant can often be found growing on sunny walls throughout the area.

Porch, Bolton-by-Bowland

This rampant display surrounding a cottage doorway caught the author's eye while strolling through Bolton-by-Bowland.

Bowland Knotts

North of Stocks Reservoir and Gisburn Forest the road to Clapham climbs over one of the highest points in the AONB at Bowland Knotts, a windswept heather-clad spot with magnificent views northwards to the Yorkshire Dales National Park and the Three Peaks on a clear day. The depth of the peat overlaying the moor can be seen where erosion has stripped away the vegetation *(right)*. When moorland fires catch hold, this peat can burn for days at a depth of several feet.

Regeneration

Delicately-veined wood-sorrel flowers emerge from a carpet of dead leaves and moss-covered rotting branches. Without question, this is one of my favourite images and captures the contrast between old and new, autumn and spring, and the whole concept of regeneration.

Cottongrass

A single stalk of one of the Cottongrass family, yet to open fully. Different varieties of the species are more easily told apart by their leaves than their flowers. Cottongrass loves the boggy soils that abound on Bowland's moors.

Totridge
Below the sculpted summit of Totridge (*above and main picture right*) its slopes feature many of the classic features
of the Forest of Bowland: conifer plantation, pockets of broadleaved trees, stone walls and rolling pastures.

Opposite bottom left: Mellor Knoll (left), Staple Oak Fell (middle distance)
and the Dunsop valley (far right in distance) from the same viewpoint.

Opposite bottom right: Mellor Knoll from Burholme Bridge.

Wood-sorrel

Wood-sorrel is often an indicator of ancient woodland. Here it is found scattered thinly across the floor of a small copse in the western fringe of the AONB. Occasionally it can be found in a substantial clump when it really is one of the most beautiful of wild flowers.

Spanish bluebell
Although the actual flowers of this visitor to our shores look very similar to our native bluebells,
these are noticeably larger and form a tight bunch. The leaves, too, are much broader.

Field boundaries

This hawthorn has, at one time many years ago, formed part of a hedge and has been subjected to traditional hedge-laying techniques. Today it remains in isolation, butting up to part of an old stone wall which has almost been swallowed up by the banking.

Roots

This interesting scene was found along Marshaw Wyre where the infant river has cut away the soft peat
to reveal an extensive root system threading its way through the turf and left dangling in thin air.

From Stoops Bridge

Rivers and streams in Bowland are generally wide and shallow with low water levels, but sudden downpours change them dramatically and adjacent pastures can flood quickly.

Inspiration

This magnificent tree was found along the Wyre Way footpath where it wends its way along the edges of parkland at Abbeystead. It gives the distinct impression of being about to uproot itself and walk away. Who knows? Perhaps it might have given Tolkein, who wrote Lord of the Rings not far away at Stoneyhurst, the inspiration to create the Ents?

Langden Brook

Rarely observed as more than a trickle, Langden Brook weaves a course past Hareden and through the valley below the Trough on its way to join the River Hodder between Dunsop Bridge and Whitewell. Opposite, the long sweep of Totridge's summit ridge can be seen in the background.

Quirks and foibles
Weekend visitors mooch around this curiosity shop in Slaidburn. Many of its items on
sale have previously served their purpose in the hands of local farmers and craftsmen.

Opposite: A basket of hand tools attracts a great deal of attention.

Any old iron

This wrought iron cattle feeder is put to decorative use outside the farm at Well Brook, situated on the banks of the Marshaw Wyre where the road leads off over Cam Brow running westwards along the foot of Hawthornthwaite Fell.

Tarnbrook is the gateway to some spectacular walking but there is no parking here.

Salisbury Hall

This attractive property in Newton in Bowland looks down over the village green towards the Parker's Arms pub and Newton Bridge. For many years until very recently, the green used to be grazed by a donkey kept by a rather eccentric lady whose cottage butts onto the green. Like many visitors, I was so used to seeing it that news of its demise came as quite a shock.

Opposite: **Bolton-by-Bowland**

Another attractive garden fronting a cottage in this tiny village in the east of the AONB.

Bluebells
There are several places in the area where a sea of bluebells can be found each spring.
These images were all shot in Hinberry Wood near Abbeystead. Hinberry is a dialect word for raspberry.

A wider Wyre
By the time the River Wyre reaches the western fringes of the AONB on its way to Morecambe Bay, having assimilated the waters of Marshaw Wyre and Tarnbrook Wyre, it is beginning to look a little more substantial.

Opposite: **Human perspective**
This lovely autumnal scene is given perspective by the diminutive solitary figure in the distance.

Rich in variety
Photographed at Bowland Knotts, one of the highest points in the Forest of Bowland, these images
show just how varied the plant life of this bleak moorland can be when you look closely.

Moorland seaweed

Some of these lichens seem to have a distinct 'marine' quality which, given their simple organic structure and the fact that they've been around for millions of years, is perhaps not surprising.

Conservation at work

Bowland AONB has teamed up with the British Trust for Conservation Volunteers to organise week-long
conservation holidays doing things like hedge-laying and dry stone walling. This group included a wide variety
of ages and backgrounds. At the end of the week they entered a regional hedge-laying competition,
such was their enthusiasm for their newly acquired skills.

Spring

This stand of trees lies just off the road south of Whitewell. With a clear blue sky behind and a foreground of green and yellow, they make a splendid sight when the foliage has that peculiar warm tone during the first two or three weeks of new leaf growth.

Blanket bog
The Forest of Bowland contains large areas of blanket bog, to the extent that it has achieved international importance.

Hen harrier country
This is a landscape which manages to look bleak even on a sunny day but compensates
for it with occasional sightings of hen harriers, jewels on a drab background.

Scrub

In better soils this photograph might show a small copse but here the trees on the hillside barely reach head height. This is reminiscent of trees I've seen growing north of the Arctic Circle in Lapland except that there they only reach knee height!

Hawthornthwaite

Although, rather surprisingly, it merits a place-name on the 1:25,000 Series Ordnance Survey map, Hawthornthwaite now consists of just an estate cottage and a nearby farm. Until its demise a century ago, there was a cluster of cottages here which housed workers from the nearby bobbin mill, but the mill was destroyed by fire and the cottages deserted. *(Opposite)* Today the tulips and daffodils in the cottage garden provide an unexpected burst of colour along the short stretch of road linking Abbeystead and Cam Brow.

Who needs a compass?
This roadside tree clearly shows the
effects of the prevailing westerlies
blowing in off Morecambe Bay.

Contre jour
The delicate translucence of new
leaves in the Forest of Bowland.

Golden saxifrage
This tumbling carpet of colour, with its leathery leaves, overhangs a mountain stream for a ready supply of water.
Apparently it can be eaten as a vegetable, at least according to my wild flower guide.

Boo!
The last of a series of images involving these three sheep and the tree, an elaborate
game was played out before I finally achieved a shot I was pleased with.

Bleasdale from Delph Wood
The rolling pastures of Bleasdale, with the ridge between Parlick and Fair Snape Fell in the distance,
are typical of the undulating farmland which surrounds the upland core of the Forest of Bowland.

Pasture and upland grasses

The sharp dividing line between usable pasture and the rough grassland of the fells is clearly seen in many places.

Country retreat
This charming cottage, tucked away from the road, is something I must have driven past a
hundred times without noticing because it is on a stretch of road where drivers need to be watching
other things. It is a perfect example of the need to get out of the car and walk.

Opposite: **First frost of the year**
The first traces of autumn frost can be seen on the grass which is shaded from the low sun by adjacent woodland.

Swollen stream, Smelt Mill

After heavy rain the streams tumbling off the fells are swollen for days as they drain the soaked peat of the fell tops.
This one drains into Langden Brook by Smelt Mill, now occupied by Bowland Pennine Mountain Rescue Team.

Opposite: **Winter colour at dusk**

People often assume that upland areas are drab places in winter. Far from it! After two days of torrential rain the
bracken and the pine needles beneath the foreground trees have become saturated with both rain water and colour.
In the low light levels approaching dusk on a dismal day, the strange luminosity of the colours was quite striking.

Marshaw Wyre in autumn

Brennands Primary School, Slaidburn
This village school serves Slaidburn and the surrounding area and was
endowed by local resident John Brennand who died in May 1717.

Ventilated dry stone wall
The capstones of this wall hang in thin air due to their perfect fit. Traditionally, no mortar is used for dry stone walling and craftsmen are adept at 'dressing' stone to ensure that each stone is a snug fit.

Renovated cottage, Newton in Bowland
Many of the cottages in the area are renovated while keeping their original features,
which usually include small windows and particularly low doors.

Elaborate cottage door, Bolton-by-Bowland
Although only a simple cottage, this has a fine nailed door complete with elaborate hinges and elegant surround.

Fishing at Whitewell

This lone figure fly-fishing downstream from The Inn at Whitewell gives a sense of scale to this deeply wooded stretch which provides a sea of colour in May due to the rich variety of tree species here.

Delicate autumn shades

Spring and autumn have to be the best times of the year to visit Bowland, with summer and winter close behind.

Bowland Pennine Mountain Rescue Team

Highly committed, specially trained and working for free – these are just of few of the volunteer members who keep us safe on the fells. Mountain Rescue Teams receive no government funding yet are relied on by the other emergency services for their specialist knowledge of the area and their expertise. They routinely provide support for events like fell races as well as being on call for emergencies.

Looking east
Established tracks can provide safe and clearly defined routes through difficult terrain and are easy to follow when mist descends.

Looking west

The same track, looking in the opposite direction, starts to be become less distinct as it enters the heart of the fells. Where paths are less defined, and especially on Access Land where paths may not exist at all, it is essential that walkers are properly clothed and know how to use a map and compass.

The Court House, Bolton-by-Bowland
This magnificent property dates from 1704 and used to house both the court and cells. The court was held upstairs on the right, with the cells at ground level below it.

The Hark to Bounty inn, Slaidburn

This legendary inn also used to serve as the location of the Halmote Court which settled local disputes in the separate upstairs courtroom. Today it is better known for its excellent lunch menu.

No longer an inn
Across the road from the Hark to Bounty lies Slaidburn Youth Hostel, formerly The King's Head.

Whortleberry, Blaeberry or Bilberry
This woody plant likes to cling to crevices in the gritstone and is seen here on the windswept summit of Bowland Knotts.

Clitheroe

While not in the Forest of Bowland itself, Clitheroe is probably the most important gateway into the area from the east.

The Trough
The road from Dunsop Bridge winds through the sweeping landscape as it climbs to its high point.
The Pendle Witches were transported along this road on their way to stand trial in Lancaster.

Opposite: **Abbeystead**
This village is a loose collection of estate properties built in similar architectural
style and has a village school but nothing else in the way of amenities.

Shades
The range of leaf shades which just one tree can provide on any given day in autumn never fails to surprise.

Opposite: **Roots and leaves**
Thick tree roots weave in and out among the carpet of rust-coloured
leaves and nuts which are strewn across this woodland floor.

Unwelcome

If the sign on the gatepost isn't sufficient to deter ramblers, someone has made sure that there are sufficient alternative hindrances to bar passage.

Welcome
A clear footpath sign and welcoming stile complete with daffodils is the order of the day.

Yellow pimpernel
A solitary burst of bright yellow enlivens this woodland floor.

Marsh marigolds
Hinberry Wood near Abbeystead has a number of small ponds in the valley,
most of which have these colourful marigolds with their large flat leaves.

Stocks Reservoir

Located on the north-east side of Bowland, this reservoir was created by flooding the valley containing the small community of Dalehead. The scattered dwellings and farms were lost for eternity but the church was rebuilt on higher ground adjacent to Gisburn Forest.

Follow the yellow brick road

Well, the sand-coloured stony track anyway. Running parallel to Langden Brook below it, this is a popular route for birdwatchers as it provides ample roadside parking and easy walking with the promise of hen harriers into the bargain.

Moorland colour
The gritstone outcrops and boulders on fell tops like Bowland Knotts are
home to a variety of lichens which fill every crack and crevice.

Primrose

Contrasting sharply with the dull grasses around it, this magnificent clump
of primroses was an added bonus on an otherwise dull day.

Tulips at Newton in Bowland

This colourful display was found at the bottom end of the village opposite the Parker's Arms and to the front of Newton Hall.
The vintage car was sheer luck. It arrived mid-shoot, its owners intent on a cooling drink in the beer garden opposite.

Pedal power
The area is a firm favourite with cyclists, particularly the Lancashire Cycleway.

Raw power
Bowland is also loved by motorcyclists. The vast majority cruise gently and considerately though it's unusual to see a lone motorcyclist like this.

Favoured spot
This pond lies just off the road on the north side of Hawthornthwaite Fell which runs over Cam Brow, to the south of Abbeystead, as it heads towards Marshaw. It is one of my favourite places to park and do some bird watching.

Storm clouds

On this particular day a series of intense localised storms passed over during a period of about three hours. This image was captured between bouts of torrential rain when visibility was reduced to a matter of yards.

For those old enough to remember
Constructions like this one at the bottom the garden were the norm, along with carefully torn pages of the
Daily Mirror suspended by a loop of string. If you're too young to know what I'm talking about, be grateful.

Main street
Slaidburn's main street on a damp winter's day.

Bridge over the River Wyre

Constructed by a lot fewer men than the one in a certain film with a similar title, this appears suddenly as one approaches through woodland from either side of the river.

Beacon Fell
Bowland Visitor Centre can be found at Beacon Fell, where there are also several waymarked walks and café/toilet facilities. Forestry operations on a small scale make use of the larch and other species which form the managed woodlands and plantations here. Local timber is used for making gates, stiles and signposts as part of the sustainable tourism programme.

Worm's eye view
Always on the look out for a different vantage point, these springtime shots of woodland were taken flat on my back!

(Opposite) The very heart of Bowland has a true sense of wilderness.

Tarnbrook

This farming hamlet lies at the head of a lane running alongside the Tarnbrook Wyre and is on one of the author's favourite walks taking in both Marshaw Wyre and Tarnbrook Wyre and Abbeystead. From Tarnbrook you can take the track through Gilberton Farm and over the ridge to Marshaw. You can also follow a different track which leads to the Black Side of Tarnbrook Fell and the White Side of Tarnbrook Fell opposite.

Short back and sides
This immaculately clipped beech hedge was found in Bleasdale.

Frosty morning

These frosted leaves appear to show signs of 'tar spot' which is a fungal disease which tends to attack the maple family and disfigures the leaves but doesn't seem to weaken the tree itself. It is highly susceptible to sulphur dioxide in the air, but as that has become less prevalent in the North-West atmosphere due to clean-air legislation so tar spot is on the increase.

Bleasdale Church serves a predominantly farming community.

Gorse

Not particularly widespread in Bowland except, perhaps, along the Dunsop valley north of Dunsop Bridge and in parts of Bleasdale, gorse is used here as part of a hedgerow which is unusual.

Silver birch
These silver birch are used very
effectively as an attractive screen to
hide the less attractive conifer
plantation behind them.

Rural life

All the images on these two pages were photographed while strolling along Slaidburn's main street. There are few places in the UK where you will find farming spilling over into village life quite so ostentatiously. Another candidate in the region is Pendleton, at the foot of Pendle Hill in the outlying part of the Forest of Bowland AONB, which has five farms along its short single street.

River Dunsop

One of the easiest but most enjoyable walks in Bowland follows the River Dunsop upstream along the United Utilities access road above Dunsop Bridge. It provides a wealth of different scenery and habitats and, at its northern end, leads to one of the most compact hanging valleys in which lies Brennand Farm. This route is classified as a bridleway so it can also be followed on horseback or bicycle.

Imperfect Bowland

Readers of my previous book *The Forest of Bowland &
Pendle Hill* often comment that the photographs
in it always depict the area in glorious weather.
Well, these images are for you!

River Hodder at Newton Bridge
Some of the best riverside walks can be found along different stretches of the River Hodder – but not today!
From Newton Bridge there are footpaths on both sides of the river which are popular with visitors and locals alike.

Grounded
Bowland has its own gliding club, situated near the village of Chipping and close to the foot of Parlick Fell, soaring over which you can often see both gliders and hang-gliders and from the top of which parascending enthusiasts take off.

Afternoon tea
One of the great rituals among cyclists is the rest at a local tearoom, in this case at
Bolton-by-Bowland where fresh scones and jam are on the menu.

More hearty fare

This café near the bridge at Slaidburn is a popular lunch stop, not least because the village car park is adjacent to it and there is a green opposite which leads down to the river. In spring the green is yellow – with daffodils.

Farmers' markets

There is a substantial amount of publicity given to local produce as it is seen as one of the main ways of promoting the area as a whole. Beef, heather-reared lamb and local cheese are just some of the area's products which are given prominence on pub menus and at farmers' markets.

Bleasdale

Set in a small copse in the heart of Bleasdale is a unique archaeological site dating back to approximately 1700 BC. This Bronze Age timber circle consisted of two concentric rings of posts, the outer one being nearly 50m in diameter. The inner circle was half that size, using 11 oak posts. What makes the site unique is that cremated human bones in two decorative urns have been discovered within the inner circle. Cremation urns and timber circles exist elsewhere but no UK site has them both in combination.

Milestone
Situated west of Dunsop Bridge at the junction of the road over the Trough and the road to Whitewell, this milestone dates from 1739.

Opposite: **Line**
One of the things I love about Bowland is the way in which you can use the landscape's sweeping lines to compose photographs.

Copse

There are many small copses in Bowland, though few are managed as coppices in the traditional sense. This one stands on a small knoll which adds to the impression that the trees are soaring upwards.

Into the light
This near-silhouette was recorded simply because I liked the shapes of the trees.

133

Common dog violet (*also left opposite*)
This delicate little violet, dwarfed by two pine cones, can be found widely in Gisburn Forest.

Early purple orchid

One of our more common orchids which flowers from April to June. It seems to enjoy the close company of bluebells in a woodland setting and at one time its tubers were thought by some to be an aphrodisiac.

Porch

This unusual front door and canopy can be found on a cottage in Bolton-by-Bowland, not far from the Court House. It is like nothing I have ever seen in the region and one day I shall discover the story behind it.

Tribute
This war memorial in Slaidburn made a dramatic picture against a sky which provided fast-changing shapes and tones. The figure is deliberately a near-silhouette to keep the mood sombre with just enough detail to make out the uniform and equipment.

Beacon Fell

The slopes of Beacon Fell are a popular venue for sledging following a decent fall of snow,
something that seems to be more and more rare even here.

Winter landscape
Snow at such low levels is unusual, seen here looking across Bleasdale towards Parlick.

Weir, River Wyre
At the western end of the reservoir at Abbeystead lies this wonderful curved weir.
The face of the weir is cobbled so the water flowing down it makes intricate small wave
forms which make a captivating sight in bright sunshine as they catch the light.

Reflection
The mirror smooth surface of this pond provided a perfect reflection of these trees.

Contrast
As I peered over the side of a bridge to look at the culvert beneath, I was struck
by these contrasting colours, shapes and movement – or lack of it.

Full stop

This woodland scene near Whitewell seemed a fitting way to end this collection of photographs. It has a finality about it,
a sort of arboreal full stop, that I can't explain so I'll have to let the image itself do the talking.